The Heart of Meditation

An Introduction to Formless Meditation Practice

Awakened Heart Sangha

Published by

The Shrimala Trust

Criccieth, Gwynedd UK

www.ahs.org.uk

Email: office@ahs.org.uk

First published December 1998

Sixth Edition: February 2015

Dear Reader,

The material you are looking at belongs to the corpus of 'Living the Awakened Heart' training materials produced by the Awakened Heart Sangha.

We publish these materials with the wish to benefit anyone seeking a valid path to Awakening.

Books alone cannot provide this.

Receiving the full benefit from the teachings requires formal transmission and direct one to one involvement with Dharma teachers and spiritual friends, the living flame of inspiration passing from one person to another.

This involvement allows you to check your understanding and make sure you are on the right track. It supports your progress and helps you to go deeper. More importantly, working closely with others helps you avoid the many side-tracks and dangers of the spiritual path. Meaning is not a solitary matter but is intrinsically bound up with connections and unfolds best in a collective context.

We hope that these books will draw readers to explore the teachings more thoroughly within the framework of the Awakened Heart Sangha.

The Awakened Heart Sangha offers:

- formal transmission and the adhistana power and inspiration associated with that

- a Mentor

- discussion with others practising in the same way

- a complete structured training giving a fully rounded approach to the teachings

- personal contact with senior students and practitioners

- sense of community

- retreats, live events and online courses

- access to more materials

Lama Shenpen Hookham
Hermitage of the Awakened Heart
Criccieth
North West Wales
UK

The Heart of Meditation is the name of the meditation course that links into the 'Living the Awakened Heart' training.

The reader is encouraged to work through the materials with a Mentor as part of the *Heart of Awakening* and *Living the Awakened Heart* training.

To find out more about the course or Lama Shenpen's teachings, please visit www.ahs.org.uk.

Contents

Introduction: What is Meditation?

People begin to meditate for different reasons. Maybe they want to be calmer, more relaxed, at peace, or at ease. Maybe they are curious about what Buddhism and meditation have to offer. Maybe they have a sense of being unhappy with their view of reality and want some sense of meaning or truth. Or maybe they have an inkling that there is something to discover beyond their everyday reality and are looking for answers to some of life's big questions, such as, why is there so much suffering and pain? What does death mean? What are we doing here at all?

Whatever moved you to embark on the *Discovering the Heart of Buddhism* course, it came from an urge to search for something or a wish of some kind. An integral part of the course is to explore the very urge or movement—perhaps it is even a longing in the heart— that brought you to this point, and trace it to its deepest source. Your wish to embark on a course of this kind shows that something has begun to stir within you, and that the process of awakening has begun. Meditation is the method for taking that process further.

What is Meditation?

Meditation is at the heart of Buddhism, and at the heart of the *Discovering the Heart of Buddhism* course. All the themes that you will be exploring in the course relate to meditation. By reflecting on these different themes, you will be homing in on your own direct experience. That experience is then stabilised and taken deeper through meditation. But what exactly is meditation? And why meditate?

A brief answer to this deceptively simple question is that meditation is what we say we are doing when we set time aside to become aware of our experience so that we can deepen our understanding of it. It is about learning how to be rather than doing anything.

When we say meditation, we tend immediately to think of sitting still. However, walking meditation and daily life awareness practice are equally important. The reason sitting meditation is stressed is that sitting is where we learn the discipline of using gentle precision to come back to the present experience. Unless we are sitting still doing nothing else it is difficult to notice what our minds are up to.

Sitting meditation is how we learn to deal with our mind, which is like a monkey rushing here and there, grasping after this and that. By starving our monkey mind of entertainment, a gap is able to open up in which we have the opportunity to come to know ourselves and find peace in our heart.

Over time, the combination of regular sitting sessions, walking and daily life awareness bears fruit. The mind becomes more calm and clear and, through the guidance of a good teacher, we come to understand the nature of our experience ever more deeply.

Meditation could be described as the process of coming home to what it is to be a human being, to our true nature. Through meditation we discover that this nature is extremely deep and meaningful, and we learn to trust it. In this course our true nature is described in terms of openness, clarity and sensitivity.

Where Does Meditation Lead?

The good news is that discovering, understanding and trusting the true nature of our being reveals how we can live a meaningful life and face death with courage. Ultimately, by coming to understand life, we come to understand death. This understanding is what is referred to as Awakening. Awakening lies beyond life and death in the way we think of them now, and the path of gradually understanding this in our direct experience is called the path of Awakening.

The Buddha taught that realising this true nature of our being is to be liberated from all suffering. Such a realisation must therefore profoundly affect our whole view of the nature of reality, of the Universe, of life, and of death.

To begin with, however, we might embark on the path with something less ambitious in mind. We may intuit that to become more awake and aware than we are now is worthwhile in itself. For example, much of our suffering is caused by bad habits that we ourselves recognise as unwise. It is fairly obvious, I think, that what is needed is more awareness. We need to wake up and stop causing ourselves and others suffering through our unawareness. This could be enough in itself to motivate us to take up meditation and start following the Buddha's path to Awakening.

Most of us, before we take up meditation, do not notice just how asleep we are most of the time. We tend to feel driven and trapped by life's circumstances as if everything were given and there were no room for manoeuvre. Meditation wakes us up to new possibilities for choosing how we experience our life. We have more freedom than we realise.

It is exciting to start to notice this even at the outset. What is wonderful is that as we continue with the practice of meditation, more and more possibilities open up and more qualities emerge that we hardly knew were there. The immediate effects of subtle shifts in our awareness can bring far-reaching changes in our attitude to our life.

If this is the taste of a little awakening, what must full Awakening be like?

The Buddha taught that there are qualities lying within each one of us waiting to be awakened. These qualities are limitless, and they are of unlimited benefit to ourselves and others. Meditation is the means of awakening these qualities. Even a little meditation can quickly reveal to us that we have the potential to be of some benefit to others, as well as put us on the path to find true peace and happiness within ourselves.

The Experience of the Heart and Mind

When we talk about meditation and taming the monkey-mind, it is easy to forget that meditation is most fundamentally concerned with the heart. Generally speaking, for most people heart and mind are taken as given. People seldom, if ever, stop to question what these are in themselves. It is as if we assume we know all we need to know about heart and mind. Although we seek knowledge of external, or even higher, things, and maybe even knowledge about our psychology, we seldom stop to wonder what our experience, awareness, heart, or mind are in themselves. To do so would be, for most people, a completely new venture.

Meditation is just such a venture, and it is quite astonishing how little we notice about the nature of our experience. We say things like 'a thought came into my mind', or 'I can't keep my mind on what I am doing'. But what happens when we look at what we are actually experiencing when we say things like that? For example, what is a thought? What is the mind that it comes into? What is the 'I' that cannot control the mind? What am I experiencing moment by moment?

Then again, what am I experiencing when I say 'wholehearted', or when I look for what I truly wish for in my heart of hearts? On the one hand, I know what it means when I hear this kind of thing. On the other hand, have I ever carefully explored what any of it means?

Meditation is a wonderful adventure in discovering that it is possible to appreciate, know, and understand our experience far more than we realised. This is important because experience is all we have.

Awareness of experience is the only thing that remains when everything that we have become attached to in the world passes. In fact, we only know of things in the world through our sensations and thoughts. Everything comes down to some kind of direct experience. Our world is made up of experience and thoughts about experience. We do not know anything else and we don't know anything in any other way.

So our experience is creating our whole world. Isn't experience amazing? Furthermore, our direct experience, which is with us all the time, turns out to have hidden depths that we never dreamed of. By simply practising meditation day after day, year after year, aspiring to be more awake, aware, and present in all that we do, a path opens up. We find that it leads to the liberation from suffering, and to Awakening to the true nature of reality. This liberating process is what is called the path of Awakening.

Meditation Instructions are Just Pointers

Although this booklet gives basic meditation instructions, they are merely pointers. They are not instructions in the sense of being something you have to 'do'. They are more suggestions for engaging in the right way, with the right touch. It is part of your nature as a human being to simply be, to let go of distracting thoughts, and remain in the present experience—to know it from the inside, as it were.

Therefore, meditation is a matter of being natural. It is nothing more than bringing our attention back to our immediate experience so that we can deepen our understanding of it, but this is surprisingly difficult to do.

The difficulty is in gaining conviction that this is worth devoting one's time to, and that it could be as simple as that. This requires persistence. We are so used to making things difficult for ourselves that we find it almost impossible to trust that simplicity, and then to remain simple.

The Two Processes of Formless Meditation

We call the type of meditation we teach 'formless sitting meditation'. This term is used to distinguish this particular practice of naturalness, which is very deep and simple, from meditation practices using images, imagination, and rituals of various kinds.

Formless meditation is the essential practice that everyone who wishes to Awaken has to do in the end, whatever method they might use from time to time. Maybe a better name for this kind of practice is 'resting in the Awakened Heart'. However, that doesn't mean much when we first set out to meditate. At least calling it 'formless' gives a sense of what it is not. It is about simply resting in experience itself, without focusing on any particular form or object.

Formless meditation involves two processes. One process is calming and settling the mind. The other is developing insight or understanding. The first is known as Shamata (calm) and the second as Vipashyana (insight).

It is the Vipashyana aspect of the meditation that leads to Awakening. Although Shamata practice brings stability through focusing on the present moment and might therefore lead us to feel more alert and awake, Shamata practice alone does not involve deep understanding. It does not liberate us from the prison of our habitual thought patterns. So the Buddha's special method is all in the Vipashyana, the development of insight. Vipashyana is the process of realising the significance of what is happening in our experience and noticing how to free ourselves from the habits of mind that trap us in suffering.

Some teachers and some meditation traditions only teach Shamata. Shamata alone can feel a bit dull and lifeless, as if it were not going anywhere. It can also feel quite wearisome because you have to work hard at maintaining a state of peace. Nonetheless, Shamata can also be enjoyable, and if it is strong enough, it can bring some special experiences, even quite amazing experiences of vastness, space, bliss, and clarity. However, these experiences come and go. They ultimately leave us where we were, lost and confused. The Buddha practised Shamata before he discovered the true way to liberation. It is important for all of us to have some experience of Shamata as a foundation for Vipashyana practice. The formless meditation I teach is a combination of calm and insight, Shamata and Vipashyana. Teaching them together like this is typical of the Dzogchen and Mahamudra tradition that we are following.

On the eve of his Awakening, the Buddha remembered that as a child he had slipped into natural meditation under the rose-apple tree, and it occurred to him that rather than the effortful practices he had been struggling with for years, he should simply rest with the confident ease with which he had meditated as a child. That is how deep liberating understanding finally arose in him and how he gained Enlightenment.

Like the Buddha, we inevitably start off by trying to create an artificial simplicity, which never really quite works, until finally we manage to stop interfering in the process of getting in our own way, as it were. This is how understanding happens. It comes out of the blue and doesn't happen because of anything we do. We nonetheless have to keep bringing our attention back to the naturalness of our immediate experience.

Simply touching on that naturalness for a fraction of a second can allow pennies to drop, and the significance of what we're experiencing can start to dawn. A natural response bubbles up, and some kind of understanding can emerge that reveals qualities and depths that we had been unaware of until that moment.

Meditation is fundamental to *Discovering the Heart of Buddhism*. The various aspects of *Discovering the Heart of Buddhism* are all for the purpose of supporting and deepening your meditation, and as you progress through the course, you will be guided through a systematic process of exploring and reflecting on different facets of your experience.

How to Practice Daily Life Awareness

Although we have been talking about meditation as the heart of Buddhist practice, perhaps it is more accurate to say that awareness is the heart of Buddhist practice. As well as meditation, this encompasses daily life awareness practice, which is sometimes called mindfulness or remembering; to remember to turn our full attention onto our immediate experience.

In a sense, we are aware all the time. We are never without awareness. Awareness is all that we are and all that we have. Experience always involves awareness. But we do not always remember to turn our attention to what we are experiencing. In order to do so, we need to keep waking up. So the daily life awareness practice is to remember to wake up to our immediate experience as often and as clearly as we can. This applies in the sitting and walking meditation as well. Our main problem, once we have started on the path, is to keep remembering our awareness practice.

We need to remember both to wake up to our immediate experience and to integrate whatever we learn from doing this into our whole way of being. This is done by remembering what we have learned and reflecting on its significance again and again.

This kind of remembering is a meditation practice in itself, and we call it daily life awareness practice. It doesn't come easily to most of us, so we have to keep finding ways of reminding ourselves, such as by reading and listening to inspiring teachings and resolving again and again to try to be more awake and aware.

How to Support Your Practice Everyday

The way we live our life in general provides the foundation for our meditation practice. An open-hearted, generous, and kind attitude to oneself and others leads to positive actions and habits of thought that feed into the meditation, and the meditation feeds back into this kind of attitude to life. If we are always unquestioningly getting involved in actions that harm ourselves and others and distract us away from the path to Awakening, then it's very unlikely we will get much benefit from trying to meditate.

A disciplined person who can keep to what they say they will do will find they can set up a regular meditation practice relatively easily. Without this kind of regular practice it is hard to get going.

On the other hand, by starting to meditate regularly, even if only for a five minute interval several times a day, that ability to discipline oneself can improve one's daily life.

Not reacting with impatience is another quality that is important both in one's daily life and as a support for the meditation. It is also a quality one learns in meditation. If we react to every little setback, thinking that we cannot practice meditation because of this or that problem, we will never get much benefit from it. We need to learn to keep going through thick and thin.

So when we become serious about our meditation practice, we need to take a good look at how we are living. We need to make our way of life the support for our meditation, and then bring the fruits of meditation into our life, for our own sake and for the sake of others.

Traditionally, Buddhist teachings emphasize the importance of making a strong connection with the Buddha, Dharma (his teaching) and the Sangha (his followers) before starting to meditate. However, I believe that these days people need to dive straight into meditation to discover its value for themselves. This, then, might give them the impetus to learn more about the Buddha and his teachings. In my view, training in meditation is the way to gain some first hand experience that would encourage us to have faith in the path.

Buddhist teachings also traditionally begin with exhortations to right living as a foundation for the path. How we behave is very important, but I find that it is most effective to let people discover this through their meditation practice. Meditation is the means by which we learn to recognise the inherent openness, clarity and sensitivity of our true nature. With perseverance we learn to trust this, and our behaviour naturally becomes more humane, generous, kind, honest, and open. It is a spiral learning process. As we are more mindful and humane in this way, the meditation naturally deepens. In other words, right living follows on from meditation just as much as meditation is founded on right living.

Part I

Chapter 1: The Essence of Meditation

Before looking at the instructions for sitting meditation that follow, I suggest you pause at the end of this section and reflect the essence of meditation. These essential aspects of meditation apply equally to the sitting, walking and daily life practice.

As I have pointed out already, meditation is about not doing anything. The act of focusing on the body and/or the breath are not the essence of meditation. They are just a means for setting yourself up so that meditation can happen. The actual essence of the meditation practice can be summed up as:

- Wake up into your immediate experience

- Connect to the heart

- Be fully present

- Open out into space

You could use the words, wake, heart, be, open as a phrase on their own, possibly repeating them from time to time to remind yourself of what the practice is about.

Wake Up Into Your Immediate Experience

"Wake up" in this context means letting go of doubts about whether your experience is good enough and accepting it as it is. Even if you feel puzzled and unsure, that is good! It's a sign you are awake. Be as bold, confident, and as trusting as you can be as you wake up to your immediate experience.

Wake up means to take your seat with confidence, with a sense of uplift and dignity, sitting up straight, being aware of your physical presence in a relaxed way. This helps settle the mind and brings you into the immediacy of your direct experience, right here and now, in a calm, stable, and integrated way.

If you are inspired by the thought of the Buddha on the eve of his Awakening, remember how he had the confidence that he could become fully awakened right there and then. He already had everything he needed in his direct experience.

Connect to the Heart

Whether you are using the physical body or the breath as the main focus for bringing the attention back when it wanders, from time to time connect to the heart as you do that. This might mean bringing yourself back from being too much in your head.

'Connect' here means remembering that you have a heart. In other words, as you try to focus on the experience of being awake right here and now, do not forget the heart. Let yourself breathe from the heart and let go from the heart, without any particular agenda.

Connecting to the heart might bring up for you a blank feeling, a puzzled feeling, or a dead feeling. It might bring up a warm and joyous feeling, a painful, tense or blocked feeling. It might bring up an open and contented feeling. It really doesn't matter what the feeling is. The point is to remember that you have a heart, and that it matters.

I don't mean by this that you should make a big project out of trying to feel anything in particular in your heart. I just mean making the heart your starting point, in a more or less physical sense. Let your awareness pause for a moment in that place where it goes when you think of what 'heart' means to you in experiential terms. It is almost like letting yourself be touched in the heart.

It is important to explore your experience and your associations with the heart in some depth. This is because all experience happens in awareness, and awareness includes the whole of our being. Since the heart is at the centre of our being, it's essential not to leave it out of our practice.

For example, when we say 'mind' or 'awareness', we might imagine some mental faculty up behind the eyes somewhere. It is important to loosen up that kind of concept and consider awareness as the whole of our experience. The heart is always integral to that whole, no matter what the present feeling in the heart happens to be.

So for a brief moment, as you wake, remember your heart and be as present as you can with the whole of your being, without trying to rush on, make something happen, change things, stop things, or decide this is good or all bad. Let whatever happens happen while being as aware of it as you can.

Be Fully Present

Of course, to wake to our immediate experience and connect to the heart already means being present. These are all different ways of saying the same thing. The important point now is to keep reminding yourself gently to be as fully present as you can and to be aware of the whole of your experience. Do this in a light way, sometimes focusing on one aspect, sometimes another. For example, you could spend some minutes bringing your awareness into the body (see below and also the body scan exercise on p. 39 for details). You could also become aware of the whole environment and sense the spaciousness of it. Or, you could allow your awareness to focus on a particular sensation coming through the senses, or on a particular feeling, emotion, or thought and sense the space in which all that is occurring.

Open Into Space

We always have a certain sense of space, even if it is a sense of feeling cramped and oppressed. The essence of meditation is to let that sense of space open up. This happens by letting go of the thoughts and feelings that seem to crowd the space. We can do this to some extent at any time, but we do not realise just how far this could go.

This aspect of the essence of meditation is discussed more in the section on sitting meditation.

Each of These Four Points Implies the Others

Although each of these four points are in fact different ways of saying the same thing, each has a unique flavour and you may find that you want to focus on one point more than another at a particular time. When any one of these four points takes you immediately to the same place as the other three, you have discovered the essence of the practice. This means, for example, that as soon as you say 'wake', you spontaneously connect to your heart, be fully present and let go into space, even if only momentarily.

'Wake up' is the instruction for those moments when we notice we are drifting. 'Wake up' is not heavy, like a job of work we have to do. It is not complicated. As soon as we think it, somehow we are doing it. It is like a sudden burst of focused energy coming from nowhere. It is a bit like suddenly being put on the spot. Someone might have just said to you 'Who are you?' or 'What are you doing here?' and you suddenly wake up out of whatever it was that you were thinking and become fully present.

Shocks have this kind of effect. Lama Rigdzin Shikpo likes to use the example of a tray of cutlery being dropped right behind you. There is a burst of focused energy that cuts through the whole thinking process and forces us to wake up into the immediacy of the present experience. That is what 'wake up' means here.

Sometimes, saying 'wake up' can pull one out of oneself. In a sense this is good and feels right, but if one is not connecting to the heart, the waking up can be somewhat heady. It can be alert and awake, but somehow it doesn't have enough meaning or significance to really satisfy. So that is when it is important to reconnect to the heart.

Being fully present implies that your awareness is in the heart and that you are awake and opening out, not closing down.

Opening into space implies being awake and present and opening out from the heart. It implies all four points.

Chapter 2: Sitting Meditation

In this chapter you will find the basic instructions for formless sitting meditation. First I describe how to set yourself up for a meditation session, which involves collecting yourself and coming into the present. Then I give instructions for the main part of formless sitting meditation and offer some advice on how to work with them.

Setting Yourself Up

Begin by deciding how long you are going to sit and resolve to keep to that. Sit comfortably, alert and relaxed. For those of you who would like some more specific advice about how to hold yourself physically, I give some suggestions in a later section.

As you settle into your meditation session, remind yourself of why you are doing it. At first this might be curiosity about what meditation is or about what might happen. Whatever your motivation, it has arisen from wanting clarity and understanding. It has arisen from some kind of weariness at the constant struggle of life. Maybe you are tired of feeling constantly driven, trapped, lost, unclear, confused, afraid, in pain. You might be tired of feeling helpless in the face of so much suffering of ourselves and others.

Meditation is about waking up out of all of that into the stark simplicity of your immediate experience, opening from the heart and being fully present to respond in an open and honest way. This is what it means to come alive, to wake up to our full potential as a human being. There is more to us and our experience than we realise, and meditation is the path to discovering that.

Next, simply wake up and become aware of what you are experiencing right now. Let go of the past and let go of the future. Wake up as if this were the first (or last) moment of your life. We can wake up and be aware because we have awareness and we have our experience that appears in it. That is all we need, so it is up to us to be bold, awake, and alert.

Be fully present and turn towards all your experience with interest in an open-hearted, confident, and easy way. Every experience, even quite subtle shifts in your perception, is worthy of attention, so you need to be fully present, meeting each experience as if it were a guest, not rejecting or ignoring anything.

Help yourself to become fully present by exploring your experience of the physical body. Become fully aware of your physical presence, starting from the sensation of your buttocks on your seat and then moving on through the whole body. This may mean noticing tension, such as around the belly, ribs, shoulders, neck and face. It may mean noticing a sense of ease and comfort, or a sense of pain and discomfort. Whatever it is that you are experiencing, it is essentially awareness itself being aware of something appearing in awareness right here and now. It is nothing more and nothing less than that. This is what we are going to explore ever more deeply as the practice progresses.

After a few minutes, when you have a good sense of your physical presence, let yourself become aware of the breath. Gently notice the rhythm of the breath as it goes in and then goes out. Every time your attention wanders off, gently and firmly bring it back to the rhythm of the breath again and again.

Paying attention to the breath can be very grounding. As long as we live, it is there, it links the body, the environment, and the movement of awareness itself as it plays between the inner and outer spheres of our experience. Relaxing around the simple movement of the breath can be a very integrating and stabilising experience.

If you are too heavy-handed as you do this, you will find yourself getting tense and having even more thoughts. So be gentle with yourself and don't let it get complicated. Train yourself to remember to keep coming back. You might find it helps at first to count the breaths up to five or ten and then start again.

Do not regard the experience of having wandered off as a problem. By bringing the attention back to the breath, you are helping to calm the mind, ready to start making friends with your immediate experience. The point is to use the sense of the breath to wake up and come into the present moment, letting go of wandering thoughts and coming back again and again. This implies that you will find yourself wandering off again and again. So treat the wandering as part of the whole experience of meditation. It is not a problem.

Developing Your Sitting Meditation

These instructions for setting up the meditation are something that it normally helps all of us to do at every meditation session. You may wish to spend several weeks setting yourself up for the meditation by practising coming back into the present and exploring your immediate experience in the various ways suggested, both in this section as well as in the earlier section on the Essence of Meditation.

Detailed Instructions for Formless Meditation

At some point, when you feel ready, move on to the main part of the meditation as outlined here.

These instructions provide a way of using the out-breath to work with the essence of meditation and they give some advice on working with the thoughts that come up in meditation. For the sake of simplicity, I particularly emphasise letting go into space, but you could equally well use any of the four aspects of the Essence of Meditation introduced earlier.

More detailed explanations of the various aspects of the main practice found here follow much later in the section on Deepening Your Practice.

Letting Go Into Space on the Out-breath

Having become aware of the rhythm of the breath as part of setting yourself up, let go into space on the out-breath.   There is no particular instruction for the in-breath. Let it happen naturally.

'Letting go' suggests different things to different people, and it's important that you don't fixate on the words in too literal a sense. What is meant by letting go is both letting go of distracting thoughts and also relaxing and opening out into the natural space of awareness.

Think of the movement of letting go as opening a tight fist. You are not actually grasping anything, but your fist is tightly closed on itself. What has to happen for it to open?   All that is needed is a very subtle change in attitude.   You allow the hand to open.   You don't actually have to do anything. You may find you prefer to say to yourself, 'open out into space on the out-breath' or, 'let be in the space of awareness on the out-breath'.

The mind is wild and wilful and needs taming, so much of the time it is very difficult to let go into the space of awareness.   It helps to have an instruction such as, 'come back to the out-breath' to keep focused on the meditation and stop drifting off, getting lost in thoughts.

Telling yourself to 'let go into space on the out-breath' helps you come back to the same spot again and again. This happens because you make a conscious decision before you start to bring your awareness back to the out-breath whenever you notice that you have drifted off.   At first, you may find that it is about as much as you can do to remember to keep coming back before you are off again into some other thought.

Be very clear about your intention, and be very firm and precise about letting go of distracting thoughts. Yet, at the same time, be gentle and relaxed about letting go, opening out, and returning to the breath again and again.

Once you are more settled, you may begin to wonder what exactly is meant by 'letting go into space' or 'opening out' or 'space of awareness' in this context. That kind of wondering is a sign that you are ready to go deeper and seek further instruction.

What if Focusing on the Breath is a Problem?

It is not a fault in the meditation to forget the breath if, instead, you are letting go into the space of awareness. It is not a fault to let go into space on the in-breath. So you can afford to have a light touch. In fact, it is essential to have a light touch. However, some people do not find focusing on the breath relaxing. It can even cause some people anxiety. So this emphasis on the breath is only for those who find that it helps them relax and focus.

The practice is not about regulating the breath or controlling it in any way. So if you find that your breath starts to become irregular by focusing on it, stop focusing on it and feel grounded in your body and the sensations associated with sitting.

To bring your attention to the immediacy of the present, it is fine to use the exact experience of whatever sensation, thought, or feeling that has appeared in the space of your awareness instead of the breath. At first this might mean you use some particular physical sensation, such as the pressure where your buttocks or legs rest on your seat, until you reach some level of calm or stability. Then, as you notice, for example, that you are thinking something, use this awareness of a physical sensation to bring you right into the present and then let go into a sense of space around that experience. Whatever it was that has appeared, if you do not follow it or try to push it away, it will dissolve by itself. It appears in space and dissolves into space and so you can rest in that space as it dissolves. It is no different from letting go into space on the out-breath.

The practice is to stay with the immediacy of your present experience, letting it go naturally into the space of awareness. When you notice you have wandered and got lost in thought, simply come back. Whatever thought that has grabbed you, just attend to it and let it go. Return to whatever sensation in your body and mind is occurring right now.

Whether you're working with the out-breath or with whatever sensation is appearing, keep a light touch. The important point is to use it to come into the present, and then to let go into a sense of space.

Working with thinking

What often happens, maybe within seconds of starting to meditate, is that we encounter thoughts that quickly whisk us away and we forget about meditation. Although the instructions are about how to let go on the out-breath into the space of awareness, when we come to it, most of the time we are lost in thoughts, chattering on to ourselves. What an amazing array of thoughts and feelings! Don't look on this as a problem. It is an important discovery. It is a sign of progress that you are beginning to notice this.

Often we find ourselves lost in the past or the future, not really noticing how this is all just thinking in the present moment. We gradually come to notice that we are driven by whatever mind-state we happen to find ourselves in, constantly making judgements and deciding for or against things and experiences. Noticing this is another sign of progress.

The instruction is not to stop thinking, but to let go of thoughts. The instruction is to help us relax and leave thoughts to play in the space of awareness without our getting lost in them.

Even if the mind wanders into a thought a hundred times, you simply notice that a hundred times. You may find it helps to label it 'thinking' as you gently bring your attention back to the breath.

It is important to recognise that the moment you become aware of your wandering mind is a moment of awake-ness. It doesn't matter if your entire meditation session consists of thinking and moments when you notice thinking with very little time actually spent on the breath. This is more of less to be expected at this point. It is the waking up that is important. All those moments of waking up add up.

Even if you have been off wool-gathering for a long time, or completely lost in an intense thought, emotion, or sensation, the instruction is the same: as soon as you notice that the mind has wandered, label it 'thinking' and gently bring your attention back to the breath. However long or short, whatever its content, it is still 'thinking'.

What is important is to get the right touch as you come to and wake up, as you connect to your heart and become fully present, and in the way that you open into space as you return to the breath. It doesn't matter how many thoughts you have or what those thoughts are about.

How To Make Use Of Meditation Instructions

There is a certain irony in the whole idea of meditation instructions. They seem to be about how to "do" meditation. But meditation, as I said, is about not doing - like releasing the grip of a tight fist. As mentioned earlier, 'let go into the space of awareness' means exactly the same as 'connect to the heart, 'be fully present', or 'wake up. You can't have one without the others because they are different ways of saying the same thing. Yet at different times, because of the way we think, one turn of phrase speaks to us more effectively than another.

There is no hard and fast rule about how to use the instructions. We naturally keep trying the different instructions and apply them to our experience in different ways. We learn by exploring and varying the instructions to discover what works. We play with the instructions in our own particular way as we try to get the right touch. In the end we have to trust our own inner sense of rightness.

There is a kind of simplicity to that sense of rightness. It is what tells you that you have found the right direction and it is what communicates to you a sense of well-being and appropriateness.

In general, we follow the instructions by gently telling ourselves to 'let go into space on the out-breath'. Then, gradually, we may find we are dropping that instruction and focusing more on waking to the immediacy of our experience. Alternatively, we may find we are dropping the instruction of 'wake up' and focusing more on 'letting go into space'.

It is good to go with what is happening and what feels right without constantly criticizing yourself or wondering if it is right or not. You are not trying to conform to some outside standard of right or wrong. You are trying to find the way forward for yourself within your own experience. The instructions are simply hints and reminders. They are not literal truths of some kind. You could use other instructions altogether if they got you to the same place.

In other words, whatever you do with any of these instructions, don't get too heavy-handed with them. The crucial thing is not in the following of the instructions, but in getting to where they are pointing. It is like map-reading. The point is not to be able to learn the map, but to discover how it relates to the situation on the ground.

In the end it is important to focus more on your own experience than on the instruction. If the instruction doesn't help you to link into your actual experience, then it is not working. You need to ask for more guidance. Tell you Mentor or teacher what you are finding. What you are finding is valid because it is your experience. The question is how to talk about that in a way that takes you deeper. Because the process is multi-faceted, there are as many instructions and hints as there are ways of experiencing the same thing. Because it is fundamentally all about the simplicity of our direct experience, all the hints and instructions come back to the same point.

All the pointing out instructions point to the same nature of reality, the same Buddha nature. Once we realise that nature, we can understand all the different instructions as perfectly pointing to the same thing. But before we realise that nature in a stable and unshakeable way, we find different instructions helpful at different times and in different situations.

All in all, it is hard to say how to decide on what instruction to use when and for how long. We have to learn to trust our own discernment and judgement. Nevertheless, it is helpful to talk to your teacher, Mentor, or fellow practitioners from time to time to learn from their experience and perhaps get some good suggestions on how to deepen your understanding.

Practicalities of Posture and Eyes

Traditionally, meditation instructions tend to start with posture, but I haven't introduced posture as the first instruction because I don't want students to associate meditation too strongly with the idea of sitting in a certain way. The way we sit can be very helpful and important, but we can meditate in any position. I want to get that message across first, before turning to the details of posture. The connection between mind and body is deeply mysterious and we shall be exploring this in increasing depth as we follow the path to Awakening.

If your heart is really opening, the body tends to be alive and at ease. If your meditation is half-hearted, the body tends to feel lifeless and heavy. Similarly, if the way you sit in meditation is naturally settled, focused, awake, and present, it helps the mind to be that way too.

From time to time it is good to notice your posture. When you notice how you are sitting and link into your heart with confidence, the body and mind respond naturally. Notice how the mind, heart, body connection works.

The main thing about sitting is to be comfortable, relaxed, alert, and confident. If the best way to achieve this for you is sitting in a chair, then sit in a chair. Other recommended ways include sitting cross-legged on a cushion or on a meditation stool. If you are sitting in a chair, find one in which you can sit upright. Whether on a chair or the floor you can experiment with different arrangements of cushions to find a comfortable and upright position.

If sitting is a problem, you can try practising lying down. It is a challenge trying to stay and feel awake when lying down, but if you are able to do so, this is actually a good position for meditation. You do not have to feel discouraged about it as if it were not correct. It is correct, but for most people it is quite difficult.

If you are sitting on a chair, keep your feet flat on the floor to give a sense of being grounded and, if you can, rest your back in a self- supporting position rather than leaning against the chair back. The self-supporting position carries the message of wakefulness.

It is important, however, not to force yourself into any particular posture but instead to be sensitive to the needs of your own body. Meditation is not an endurance test. It is about waking up and being happy!

For more details on both the spirit and the practicalities of posture, see the chapter called 'Posture' in Openness Clarity and Sensitivity by Lama Rigdzin Shikpo.

Key Points for Sitting Posture

Hands on thighs, palms down over knees. This is referred to as the gesture of 'calling the earth to witness'. For those familiar with the story of the Buddha, this reminds us of the Buddha calling the earth to witness on the eve of his Enlightenment. You need to check that the position feels open and relaxed for you. If you need to draw the hands in from the knees to feel comfortable that is fine. It is not a problem to have the palms together in the lap, but we favour the hands on the thighs because it is an opening out gesture rather than enclosing and inward-facing. Also it is the posture in which the great teacher of our lineage, Longchenpa, is always depicted.

- Feel the support of the ground in buttocks and legs. You don't have to dwell on this, but somehow when you have been rushing around and feel pulled out of yourself, just to bring your awareness into that connection with the good solid ground beneath you can have a surprisingly stabilising and calming effect.

- The back is long, straight and broad. Interestingly, just thinking this can physically affect how you hold your back. It is almost like giving your back permission to be what it really wants to be. The spine needs to be erect, but not rigid or strained.

- The shoulders need to be relaxed, but neither slumped (too loose) nor thrown back (too tight).

- Let the head feel suspended as if from a thread at the crown. You might imagine that a thread runs up the length of your spine, through your neck and head, out the crown of your head and is attached to the sky, gently lifting you upwards towards the sky, but without any strain or effort. This can feel literally uplifting. The rest of your body can then relax all the way down from that thread. With the crown of your head gently lifted by this imaginary thread, you will find your head naturally tilts slightly down. Your head, neck and shoulders should all be vertically aligned and feel naturally comfortable.

Eyes Open

In this form of meditation the eyes remain open, looking four to five feet ahead of you on the floor. Keep the eyes half open or fully open, whichever feels most natural. In either case, it is important to have a 'soft focus', not staring hard at anything, but just resting the eyes, rather as you might when listening intently to music or looking out of the window. It is like being aware of the world around you in your peripheral vision, but not as an object to focus on.

It may take some practice to become comfortable having your eyes open in this way, especially if you are used to meditating with them closed. But it is strongly recommended that you persevere.

The problem with meditating with the eyes closed all the time is that the meditation can become a kind of inner world you withdraw into that you have to leave as soon as you stop meditating. The entire orientation of this formless practice is to remain connected with the world around you. With the eyes open, you stay connected and open to the world.

Advice on How to Move Forward

If you are trying to get started on meditation for the first time, you might find that you now have more than enough to work with for the next week or even for the next few weeks. There is no need to hurry. Please go at your own pace and follow your own inspiration.

When you are ready to move on, I suggest you read the chapters on Walking Meditation, Daily Life Awareness Practice, Establishing Your Daily Meditation Practice, and the section on Heart Wish. Then, when you are ready, I suggest you move on to Part II, Deepening Your Practice.

Those who have meditated before or who feel inspired to read on, Part II offers more detailed instructions about how to work with thoughts and feelings that arise in meditation, and how to let go and let be in the space of awareness. This emphasis on space is characteristic of the way meditation is taught in the Dzogchen tradition. Part II helps you to deepen your practice by combining your Shamata practice with Vipashyana.

Chapter 3: Walking Meditation

Walking meditation acts as a bridge between formal sitting practice and daily life awareness practice because you have to maintain an awake and aware quality while you are moving. In the sitting practice we get used to everything around us remaining still while it's the mind that is moving. It can come as quite a shock to have to deal suddenly with all the changing sense impressions as well as the movement of the mind. Walking meditation is an opportunity to deepen your awareness practice generally. It is different from ordinary walking in that it has no other purpose than meditation, so you are more likely to remember to be aware than in going about your daily life, when you have so many things to think about.

Once you have become used to walking meditation, you might find that having to walk about automatically reminds you of the practice. You may find that taking your seat at your desk and waiting at bus stops and so on, act as triggers of awareness in a similar way. Walking meditation is a good practice to do on its own or to incorporate into the middle of a longer sitting meditation.

How to Engage with Walking Meditation

Start by finding a time and a place when you won't be disturbed, where you can walk up and down or in a circle, either indoors or out. Intend from the start for this to be a meditation session, a time when you are concerned with being in the present moment and waking up rather than a normal walk where your aim is to get somewhere, get exercise, or have an entertaining time.

Take stock of your bearing as you walk. Use your experience of your body sensations as you move to bring your awareness back when you find your attention has wandered (For help, see the Body Scan section).

Walking meditation can be a way of expressing awake, attentive awareness, a sense of freedom of movement in space, and an opening movement of the heart. It can all be there in the simple exercise of walking calmly up and down like the Buddha in the forest outside his meditation hut.

As well as the body sensations, or instead of the body sensations, you can sometimes work with all the direct sensations that come through your senses. Usually, when we sense something we immediately tend to interpret it and perceive whole solid objects. However, if you let yourself be very simple like a child who has never seen anything before and doesn't know what anything is, you tend to see colours and shapes and not be constantly identifying and naming things, telling yourself stories about them, and so on.

For example, if you hear a sound, it is pure sound and somehow a mysterious experience, but then you might immediately think 'lots of birds – I wonder what is going on – they are making so much noise, is there a cat about?' and so on. One thought leads quickly to another and you are off into speculations, past and future, judgements for or against and endless story lines that you are telling yourself. So as you walk, you simply bring your attention back to the pure sound itself. Rest in the openness of your heart and the space of your mind and notice just the sound.

This is not easy to do because we automatically add concepts, ideas, and memories to our bare experience. It is the same with tactile sensations, visual input of colour and shape, smells, and so on. As much as you can, you are trying to be as simple as possible, just noticing the pure sensations. The reason for doing this is that it is a good way of waking up and bringing our awareness right into the present experience so we can understand its nature better. As soon as you feel you have got caught up in thinking, let it go and come back to the pure sensations.

Instead of looking all about you at this and that as one ordinarily tends to do when walking, keep your gaze steady. Gently keep your attention straight ahead without letting your thoughts and senses pull you out of yourself. Take in the whole situation around you as if it were coming to you.

In brief, as soon as you notice your attention has wandered, bring it back to the immediacy of your direct experience be it the sensations and movement in your feet, the wind touching your face, the rhythm of your footsteps, or the sounds of the birds. If you can experience all this with a sense of opening your heart out into space, then all the better. As time goes on, this practice can deepen into letting go into the fundamental space of awareness beyond concepts, following the same instruction as for formless sitting meditation. In other words, it can lead to deep insight and is a wonderful way to meditate, especially if you are tired or sleepy.

Body Scan Exercise

A useful exercise, especially if you are feeling distracted and pulled out of yourself, is to begin the walking meditation with what is sometimes called a 'body scan'. That is to say, you systematically work through your whole body from the soles of the feet to the crown of your head, training yourself to keep your attention on the sensations of that particular area of the body for a few moments before moving on to the next one. You could also do this sitting or lying down. It is the same exercise as I suggest for people who find focusing on the breath a problem. You can just use the natural sensations within your body to bring your attention back when it has wandered.

If you have been quite distracted, this can help you slow down, open up, relax and come alive. It is a matter of being more awake and aware of your direct experience, right here and now, letting go of impatient thoughts about getting on, and not wasting time. You just take time to be, in this very simple way.

While walking, you could extend this exercise to the movement of the feet in slow motion. Otherwise, you could apply it to the motion of walking at a normal speed.

Chapter 4: Daily Life Awareness

Daily life awareness means waking up right here and now wherever we are. Anything could be meditation if we were sufficiently awake and aware. People often tell me they feel more awake and aware when they are busy. But that is just because things are happening that are grabbing their attention. The problem with that is that when nothing is happening, we feel bored and restless. This is a sign that our ability to rest in awareness is weak and we are depending on outer circumstances to keep us going, looking for external situations to entertain and inspire us. That is a path that goes nowhere. It means we are always at the mercy of circumstances.

In daily life awareness practice we are looking for the awake quality that comes alive right now in our own awareness, in whatever circumstance we find ourselves in. It is about taking the relaxed, confident and awake quality that we find in meditation and bringing it into our daily life, so that we live our lives, with a relaxed confidence, in that same space of awareness. The following are some hints for how you can begin to do this.

- Set up triggers of awareness in your daily routine. This means choosing things that you do regularly and then deliberately creating an association with them in your mind that will increase your chances of remembering your meditation. For example, each morning as you open your curtains you could think of Awakening. Or whenever you look at the sky you could rest in the sense of spaciousness.

- Use routine activities, such as mealtimes, walking, cycling, or brushing your teeth, as opportunities to practice meditation. You could use any sight, sound, smell, taste or bodily sensation to bring you into the immediacy of your direct experience.

- Whenever there is a gap in your activity, you could focus on the out-breath and let go into space, even as you sit at the desk, cook in the kitchen, or travel to work.

- When difficult moments arise in your life, make a point of turning toward the experience and noticing thoughts as thoughts, feelings as feelings, sensations as sensations. Or, you might find it helps to 'ground' yourself by becoming strongly aware of the sensations of your feet where they touch the ground and then bringing your attention to your breath, helping you to slow down, centre yourself, and create a gap instead of reacting too quickly. Bringing your awareness to your out- breath, connecting to the heart and letting go into a sense of spaciousness might allow a more appropriate response to bubble up before habitual reactions take over.

- During the day, periodically bring your attention back to what is happening in this very moment. Let the moment cheer you up. This is a manifestation of awareness itself, which is naturally spacious and full of strange and amazing qualities. The immediacy of your direct experience can become an endless source of wonder and delight, of new insights and glimpses of a deeper reality. So instead of mulling over the past or worrying about the future, honour the present. Relax into the spacious, awake nature of awareness that is always there.

As your understanding of heart, space, openness, clarity and sensitivity deepens, this will naturally carry over into your life. You will find you become more sensitive and respond to situations more appropriately.

I suggest you train yourself to remember the little phrase of wake, heart, be present, open, bringing it to mind when you can during the day. I think it might help you to remember to reconnect to the heart and why you are practising meditation.

The teachings I give are all designed to give you further inspiration and advice about how to meditate wholeheartedly and effectively in your daily life.

Motivation for Reflecting on the Heart Wish

In order to start to notice and let go of 'thinking', we need to sort out our priorities. We need to think about what we really want. Instead of taking a hard line with yourself, saying you shouldn't be distracted, you need to decide for yourself what is wrong with thoughts and what is good about them.

If we do not reflect from time to time about what we really want from the meditation, we can lose our motivation. We might find that we are doing it as a kind of 'should' that isn't coming from our heart, and we might even start beating ourselves up about it in a heavy-handed and judgemental way.

It is good to ask ourselves whether we want to notice and let go of thinking or not. What kind of thinking is a problem and what is not? What kind of thinking do we want to let go of and what kind of thinking is helpful? Maybe there are some habitual patterns that it would not be good to let go of. Maybe what we really want is to have the freedom to choose whether we let go or not according to the circumstances.

It is important not to let the meditation instructions bully us. Meditation has to come from our heart, and for this we need to ponder and reflect on what that means.

If we are indeed seeking the freedom of letting go of negative thinking and being able to think in a positive and helpful way, I think it is fairly obvious that we will first have to train in noticing thinking as it arises and letting it go. Maybe that is enough to inspire us to persevere in bringing the mind back again and again. It is sometimes important to reflect in this way about why we are meditating and what it has to do with what we want in our heart of hearts.

In meditation there are two processes going on in terms of thinking. One is to notice positive and negative thinking and encourage ourselves to strengthen the first and let go of the second. Meditation helps us notice what kind of thinking is going on and therefore it gives us some freedom of choice. Over time we learn that we can let go of thinking and bring the attention back to the immediacy of the present experience whenever we want to.

A second, deeper process takes over from this as we settle into the practice. This is when we notice that whatever we are thinking, good or bad, is all 'thinking' and it is all the same movement in awareness. We don't need to follow the thinking and we don't need to stop it. We can just let it be in the space of awareness.

A still deeper process follows on from this when we start to recognise what the nature of awareness and thoughts really is. Then it all gets very interesting indeed. This is what eventually leads to liberation, complete Awakening, or Enlightenment. I sometimes refer to this as the fulfilment of our deepest heart wish.

You may notice moments or flashes of understanding or significance quite early on in meditation. It is important to notice moments of an intuitive sense of meaning or significance about what you are experiencing. These are what you need to cultivate. You need to find ways of practising that bring out this sense of meaningfulness more and more.

Finding the Heart Wish

In the *Discovering the Heart of Buddhism course* there is a detailed exploration of how to connect to what we really want in our heart of hearts. It is a question of discovering for ourselves what that really means.

We often grasp onto ideas of what we think we want and chase after them, but when we stop to look, we notice the wanting is there before the ideas. The wishing or wanting itself is not ideas or thinking. It is a sense of something deeper and more constant than all of that, and this is what we need to link into and reflect on again and again.

I call this the heart wish. It is an aspect of your experience that is always there, always wishing for what is good. In fact, it is wanting what is best. However, if we do not dig deeply enough, we never realise what that best really is. We become trapped in a fruitless pursuit of lesser goals. Even if we attain them, they do not bring us what we really want.

It is so easy to become discouraged and think it is useless to seek our heart's satisfaction. Often people try to disconnect from the heart because they associate it with pain and despair. In this way people forget they even have a heart and never connect properly with their heart-wish, which is nonetheless still there. Meditation is for connecting to the heart. It is important not to forget this. For some people that might sound trite or, on the contrary, it might sound scary and painful.

It sometimes takes quite a bit of exploration and meditation before it feels natural to be truly in touch with one's heart and heart-wish. That is not a problem. In fact, we never really lose an intuitive sense of that longing in the heart and what it would feel like for that to be fulfilled. That intuitive sense is intrinsic to what it is to be alive and is what has brought us to this point of wanting to get started with meditation. It is enough to start with. You don't have to know what the heart-wish is before you start. You discover what it is as you go along.

The important point here is that meditation is about what you, in your heart of hearts, want. It is not about somebody else saying that you have to give up these negative, distracting and habitual thoughts. It is you who is deciding for yourself what you want. Opening to your immediate experience and letting go in meditation is about your freedom of choice. It has to be the way you want to go, it has to come from your heart-wish.

To really be able to rest in that completely may take a lifetime of practice, but even to rest in it momentarily has a surprisingly powerful effect and can make a whole difference to how we experience our daily life or make our life decisions.

Chapter 5: Establishing a Daily Practice

Having reflected on the heart-wish and decided that meditation is what you want to do, commit yourself to the discipline of a regular meditation schedule.

It takes conscious thought and planning to establish and maintain a meditation practice. Our initial resolve to meditate can easily be eroded by the busyness of our daily lives, by our commitments and by the force of habits pulling us in many different directions. The following are some tips to help you establish and maintain your practice:

Working with a Mentor.

Your Mentor is your living connection to the Sangha. They are available to answer questions, encourage, or make suggestions. It can often be reassuring to talk to someone who is interested in your desire to practice. This is especially true when life's circumstances and our own negative tendencies are getting the better of us!

For the first few weeks, we recommend regular weekly communication with your Mentor to discuss what you are going to focus on and review your experiences as you progress through the course.

This process helps to form a relationship with your Mentor and with the Sangha in general. It can be very inspiring to relate to others who are practising and everyone benefits when we can do that in a mutually supportive way.

Resolve

It is fairly obvious that you must have some kind of intention to do the meditation practice or it simply won't happen. What isn't so obvious is how you can strengthen the power of your intention by means of making resolves and keeping to them.

Just saying to yourself 'I think I might meditate' doesn't carry much power and it's quite likely you'll end up not meditating. However, if you bring your full mind and heart to making the intention to practice, saying to yourself, 'I make the commitment to practice 15 minutes every day for 30 days', it is much more likely that you will do it. You can seal your resolve by telling your Mentor what you have decided to do, otherwise you could tell someone close to you, especially if they are willing to call you to challenge you when they notice you are not doing it!

Regular Daily Practice

It is important to set up a regular, daily, basic routine for meditating. Meditation then becomes a part of your daily life, the way brushing your teeth does. You don't have to make a separate decision about it. You simply do it without fail.

There are the four areas of practice: sitting, walking, daily life awareness and course work, so you need to set up a daily, weekly, or monthly routine that brings it together. You can talk to your Mentor about how to set up your routine.

One suggestion might be to promise that if you do fail to keep to your commitment, you will get in touch with your Mentor to discuss it. Just the fact you will have to ring them to talk about your practice may give you the boost you need to do the practice instead.

Time of Day

Experiment to find the time of day that works best for your own schedule and temperament, and then stick with it. In this way you develop a regular daily rhythm to your practice, and it begins to run itself. Otherwise, it is all too easy for this, that and the other to push the meditation out of your day.

Length of Practice

Decide on the length of time you will meditate for and stick with that, not getting up for anything short of a real emergency. It helps to use a timer so that you can relax into the practice without worrying about time. In the beginning do not be over ambitious. It is far better to do a regular, short meditation each day than to do a marathon occasionally. Try starting with 10-20 minutes a day, but this is something you could discuss with your Mentor. If all else fails, make a resolve to do at least five minutes when you get up, five minutes at some point during the day and five minutes before going to sleep at night.

Where to Meditate

Select a suitable space for your practice where you can sit comfortably and be reasonably undisturbed. A corner of your bedroom or any other quiet spot is fine. You may find it helpful to arrange things in this space that are conducive to meditation such as your special meditation seat, inspiring readings or even a Buddha image on a shrine (see below), or anything else that inspires you personally. It could be quite inspiring in itself to create a sacred, peaceful and uplifting space in this way. It is surprising how others can sense the sacredness that builds up over time. Even animals seem to respond to it.

Shrine

You may want to make a special shrine. If so, you could look at the booklet Mandala of Sacred Space for more information about setting up a shrine. This could be a table with a picture of the Buddha and a candle, and/or flowers and incense.

Liturgy/chants

Reciting some liturgy at the start of meditation helps set one up with a sense of inspiration, context and motivation for the meditation. We have chants (referred to as liturgy) that we do together as a Sangha and you might like to do these on your own. You can find them in the booklet called Mandala of Sacred Space.

Part II

Chapter 6: Deepening Your Practice

Working with Thinking

It is tempting to feel frustrated that we are not getting anywhere when we find ourselves lost in thinking again and again. Even though we know that meditation is simply a matter of turning toward the immediate experience, if it's thinking, a feeling, an emotion or whatever, it is hard to believe that that is enough.

Instead, we find ourselves judging the meditation. Thoughts like 'This is good', 'This is no good', 'I don't want that', 'I want that', 'How can I get it?', 'How can I get rid of it?' can be going on almost every moment of the day in gross and subtle ways. It is important to notice these judgmental thoughts and recognise them for what they are. They are just thoughts.

Do not let yourself develop the attitude of 'Oh, I can't meditate because I have so many thoughts'. Instead, you need to cultivate the attitude that the thoughts themselves are contributing to the meditation. They are integral to it. Meditation gives us the opportunity to experience the power of letting go of distracting thoughts. The more thoughts we experience, the more opportunities we have to familiarise ourselves with their essential nature and to let go of them.

Each time we notice that we have become caught up in the thinking process, the instruction is to gently label it 'thinking' and return our attention to the breath. Gradually, we will come to realise that we have the power to let go or step out of any mind-state; we notice this to some extent fairly early on, but it takes long and persistent meditation to realise this fully.

How do we step out of a mind state in this way? It is not easy to say is it? We just seem to be able to do it. We have the power to switch our attention and return it to the breath in a firm, relaxed, gentle way. Even if we find we have immediately drifted or wandered off, as soon as we remember, that choice is there again. After a while you may notice that there is something quite mysterious about the way we notice we have drifted and the power of choice that is right there as soon as we remember. Starting to appreciate that is another sign of progress.

One of our problems is that we have convinced ourselves of all sorts of reasons for not wanting to let go of our habitual thinking. Perhaps there is part of us that thinks that it wouldn't do to let go of all of it. Nonetheless, it is important to notice that letting go or not is a choice, which is interesting in itself.

Furthermore, as we practise it is possible to notice that we have the power to choose to relax into the space of awareness even as the thoughts come and go.

Getting the Right Touch

If you try too hard to let go of thinking, the mind speeds up and more thoughts than ever seem to come up. If you don't try hard enough it's business as usual. Nothing changes and you discover nothing of interest. So it's a matter of getting the right touch.

One way of doing this is to adopt toward thoughts an attitude you would have toward guests at your party. Put another way, it is a matter of turning toward your experience. You are the good host who acknowledges the presence of each guest in a welcoming way, but you don't linger too long with any one of them. You move decisively on to the next one without roughly pushing the first guest aside. It is more relaxed than that. The guest comes, you notice the guest, you respond warmly and with interest, but then before getting sucked into the world of that guest, you let them go or let them be as you move your attention back to the breath or back into that movement of letting go into space.

Noticing Thought Itself Rather Than Content

When a thought arises, try to be as fully present with what that thought is in itself. The content of thought does not matter, even though this is hard to believe sometimes.

We tend to judge our thoughts quite strongly. If in our meditation we have lots of good thoughts we think, 'Oh, that meditation was good'. If we have lots of bad thoughts we think, 'Oh, that meditation was bad'. Actually, if we are judging our meditation in this way, we have missed the point. The meditation is not about whether the thought content is good or bad. The meditation is about recognising the true nature of thought in itself, regardless of whether we believe the content to be good or bad.

Bad meditation, I would say, is believing in good and bad thoughts as being real, as being what we are. Good meditation would be equanimity, where we recognise thinking as thinking and let all the thoughts be as they are in the space of awareness.

The instruction to label thinking as 'thinking' is a good way of learning this kind of equanimity. It is a way of learning to recognise all experiences, feelings and thoughts as simply experiences and essentially equal in status. Whatever they are, whether the content seems good or bad, in essence they are all simply thought, not other than the awareness in which they occur. This is very mysterious!

It would not be helpful to try to label every thought as thinking. Most thoughts come and go in the space of our awareness without any need to say 'thinking' to ourselves. However, from time to time, when you notice you have got caught up in a train of thought and completely forgotten about meditation it can be very helpful to say to yourself, 'thinking'. It is sometimes quite a shock to realise that it is indeed thinking and not the real world.

We often take our thought worlds so seriously that it is wrenching to bring ourselves out of them and recognise them for what they are. Sometimes we are so identified with our thoughts that the possibility of letting them go can feel like facing death itself. We might find ourselves thinking, 'How could all that be thinking? Isn't it my whole life? My whole past? My whole future? If I let all that go, how would I be able to live?'

When this kind of reaction comes up it is good to notice that it is thinking too. It can all be let go of as thinking in the space of awareness. That can be a very liberating experience.

The instruction to 'label thoughts as thinking' is a way to learn to step out of thought-worlds and subtly change one's perspective on them. For example, maybe we are in the middle of this lively self- justifying argument when up pops this observation, 'thinking'. We do not actually have to carry on and prove our point. We can gently acknowledge that this is merely thinking and regardless of what it was about, return to letting go into space on the out-breath.

If you find that you are anxiously watching yourself and trying to stop thoughts, recognize that also as 'thinking' and let the anxiety go. Let it be in the space of awareness. The irony is that all our anxiety and effort to control the mind isn't stopping thinking at all. It is increasing it!

While you are lost in thought, you are not awake. Then, suddenly you come to and remember you had intended to keep the attention on the immediate experience of the out-breath. When you wake up to the fact that you are thinking, it is a moment of waking up and you are back. But it happened spontaneously. You didn't do it really.

Now that you have left the thought and come back to the breath, it is important not to spoil the simplicity of that moment by thinking, even ever so slightly, 'Damn, I wandered'. Instead, be as gentle as you can and as aware as you can be of the movement from being lost in thinking to waking up, noticing the essential nature of the thought, connecting to the heart, returning to being fully present with the breath and opening into space.

The Watcher is also 'Thinking'

When we talk about meditation in terms of letting go of thoughts, it can seem as if it is a matter of setting oneself up as an observer of one's mind and to root out thinking. This is a misunderstanding of the whole process.

Setting up a watcher in this way perpetuates our false sense of what we are and what our experience is. The observer might well be well intentioned, but the problem is that it is heavy-handed and believes too much in itself. It doesn't see that it is itself another case of thinking.

Do not adopt a forceful attitude, as if you could become enlightened through sheer willpower. That kind of willpower is egocentric and controlling. It is the watcher divided from the experience trying to make it be the way it thinks it should be. When you find that kind of watcher-mentality has taken over, which often happens, turn towards it and recognise it as thinking. Let it go. It is not another part of you that is oppressing you.

Turning Toward Negative Experiences

As well as getting lost in thoughts, another thing we start to notice is that there are certain thoughts or feelings we habitually try to avoid. We might quickly push them away or deliberately discount or ignore them. We sense the thought or feeling coming up and we immediately start thinking our way out of it or dulling out in some way. For example, if we feel angry with someone we might try not to think of them.

The instruction is to turn towards persistent thoughts and feelings, recognise them as thinking, and let them go. However, there is a tendency to take the bad thoughts and feelings as real and then shrink from them, trying to find a way to avoid them. The trouble is that this intensifies the sense that they are real and something we need to escape from. We then find ourselves weaving storylines to justify and convince ourselves of the reality of our preconceived ideas. This again intensifies the thinking process. The meditative approach to this situation is to turn towards the very thoughts and feelings that we are trying to escape, acknowledge them as thinking, and let go of the storyline. There isn't anything wrong with having a story-line, but it is important to choose them carefully and not let our preconceptions, thoughts and feelings drive us as if they were real and we had no choice.

This is what it means to stay simply with the immediacy of your experience. This way you are really in touch with your experience because you allow yourself to be fully present with it however bad it may be.

First, notice the repeating storyline going on around the bad feeling. For example, one finds oneself thinking, 'She did that. I won't let it happen again. I am not going to speak to her. She always does that', etc.

Try to focus on what the actual feeling is behind all that thinking. What is the experience that drives it? Try to open and turn towards it to experience it precisely. What is it exactly? Even if you end up not being sure, just notice it and then let it go. Do this again and again.

It is interesting that when we do this we often find that it is not as unbearable as we thought it was. It may be painful and may last a long time, but when we really turn towards it and let go of our struggle to avoid experiencing it, then we can relax into it and the experience becomes much simpler. It is likely that it is not quite what we thought it was and perhaps it may be rather strange and interesting.

Turning towards experience in this way is simple and yet very hard to do especially when the experience is intense. However, there is nothing else that works on intense experiences of pain either physical or mental. Even if we find this practice hard, it is no harder than the pain itself. Struggling to avoid experiencing what one is experiencing is much worse.

Ebb and Flow of Awareness

Whatever our circumstances, every moment and every detail of our life from the moment we get up in the morning to the moment we go to bed can be a step in the path to Awakening. The discipline of becoming more aware of the experience of the moment provides opportunities to be more open, clear and sensitive.

However, there is a natural rhythm to focusing and relaxing our attention. It is important to get the right touch in regard to this. Do not try to be so focused that there is no relaxation. Instead really let go into the simplicity of awareness without trying to do anything. The focusing of awareness will happen naturally within that.

For example, although we think we are in control and could wake up at any time, we cannot apply an instruction to wake up until we have woken up enough to remember the instruction! When we apply the instruction to wake up, we must have already woken up sufficiently to remember the instruction. The 'coming to' happened spontaneously as a natural function of awareness itself. 'I' didn't do it, awareness did. It is important to notice that awareness is always moving from moments of focused attention into a more open, spread out, relaxed mode of being from which it can focus again. There has to be this kind of movement all the time for awareness to know anything.

Awareness never stays focused. There has to be a movement of ebb and flow. Something appears and awareness focuses. It is as if something from the background of awareness has come into the foreground and then moves into the background again as something else comes into the foreground. The movement into the background is like a fading, dissolving, or spreading into space, and the movement into the foreground is like a focusing or intensifying of energy. Awareness moves within itself in that way all the time, at its own pace, in and out of focus.

However long we wander we can be sure that the attention will always come back into the immediacy of the present experience at some point. In meditation we are trying to create conditions for this natural coming back to be more frequent and sustained and then to realise the significance of it.

What is the use of an instruction such as 'wake up'? Isn't this a bit too contrived? In a way it is but often, especially to start with, the phrase can nudge us to intensify our attention, to sharpen our awareness at the moment of coming to and set up conditions for it to happen again spontaneously.

For example, when we have been drifting lost in thoughts and we suddenly, out of the blue, remember we are supposed to be meditating, if at that moment we say to say ourselves, 'wake up!', that can bring us into the immediacy of our experience very sharply. We don't have to say that every time we come to. Sometimes we might come straight back into the immediacy of our experience, straight back to the breath or straight back into letting go into space. Sometimes we might simply note that thinking is thinking and let it go.

For a long time we will find we need to combine a trust in the natural movement of awareness with a bit of mental prodding to energise the process and keep ourselves on course. Eventually we will not need to prod in this way because we will be awake enough to rely solely on the natural and spontaneous movement of awareness.

Strengthening our Resolve

To train in this way we need to be convinced that it is necessary to give up getting caught in distracting thought-worlds. Otherwise whenever a thought comes up that we feel drawn into we let it take us over. Letting ourselves be taken over like this is the opposite of meditation.

Even though waking is spontaneous and we cannot make it happen on the spot, we can set ourselves up by our reflection, our attitudes, our habits and our resolves so that those moments of coming to become increasingly likely. Much of the path of Awakening is about how to set ourselves up in this way. The essential process of becoming Awakened is actually simple and happens by itself. What we need to train in is to become simple enough to allow it to happen. We need to set ourselves up in a way that is conducive to its happening. Resolving to sit to meditate in regular sessions is part of that.

Although it is important to maintain a strong intention not to become lost in your thoughts, it is the hardest thing in the world to avoid this. So it is important that whenever you notice thinking, you allow yourself to feel pleased at having come to rather than annoyed at yourself. This helps cut through the tendency to push, achieve and judge yourself negatively, which is more harmful in the end than the wandering. Be particularly alert to the voices of 'Lordly Judgment', which tell you that you are no good; you can't meditate and are wasting your time. These, too, are thinking.

Let Go into Space on the Out-breath

Once you have set yourself up for meditation and you are beginning to settle down and come into the present, it is time to begin the main part of the meditation. The main instruction at this point is to 'let go into space on the out-breath'. The following section is to help you explore what these words might be pointing to in terms of your own experience.

When you are using the out-breath to link into that 'letting go into space' movement, follow the breath out until it fades, then 'let be' in the space until the next out-breath. This instruction intuitively makes sense when you are experiencing the out-breath as slightly stronger, longer, and more relaxed than the in-breath. If you find that your in-breath is actually stronger, longer, and more relaxing, then go with that. Let go into space with the in-breath if that feels intuitively right. It comes to the same thing.

This particular instruction on how to use the breath in meditation emphasizes letting go into space. In some meditation methods the main emphasis is put on the breath, but here we use the breath as a gentle reminder and inspiration and the main emphasis is on the space of awareness. Rather than more detailed instructions about how to focus on the breath, we are told to get a general sense of the movement of the breath as it happens in space.

Not all one's attention is focused on the breath. At least half again is focused on the space of awareness in which it is happening and the simple movement of opening and relaxing into that space. That movement is actually within awareness itself. That is why you don't have to focus on the breath to focus on that movement. However, since the out-breath is generally a relaxing movement and breath is quite literally going out into space, focusing on the out-breath is naturally evocative of the kind of movement in awareness that we are talking about.

Because 'letting go' is simply a pointer and suggests different things to different people, it's important not to let the words get in the way of the experience. Use turns of phrase that bring you back to your immediate experience. It is important when we say to ourselves, 'let go into space', that we get a sense of relaxation. If that particular phrase has the wrong effect, then look for a better way of telling yourself what is needed.

It is all right to use different words or phrases, so play with the instruction a bit. When you have found a phrase that works for you in terms of getting you to a place that feels more relaxed, open and spacious, use that as your key instruction. You may find that in some moods one phrase works better than another. You can always change it.

As you practice you will become increasingly familiar with this relaxing movement in your awareness. In the end you will hardly need a word for it at all.

Some Subtle Points to Consider (bullet points?)

Gently labelling thoughts, feelings and sensations as 'thinking' is a way to learn to step out of them and subtly change your perspective on them.

Meditation is about what thoughts and awareness are in themselves. The content of thought does not matter.

Treat thoughts as guests.   Welcome and appreciate them briefly, but don't linger too long.

Turn towards difficult experiences with interest. Don't try to shrink, hide or push them away.

Don't let judgemental and 'should' thoughts drive you. Label them as thoughts and treat them like any other thought.

Awareness naturally moves in and out of focus. Appreciate the movement as you learn to wake up in the midst of it.

When thoughts, feelings or emotions absorb your attention, as you wake out of that state, reinforce you intention.

Letting go of what arises happens naturally as you wake up and return to your practice.   Appreciate this movement as stepping out of attachment.

Appreciate the sense of ease that starts to develop that is undisturbed by passing thoughts.

Appreciate how there is a fundamental quality of stability about your experience. Your experience is not just passing thoughts, feelings and sensations.

Don't try to stop thoughts. Seeing into their nature is the means to insight.

Don't cling to notions of peace and stillness as these too are thoughts.

When all the instructions become one and the same, you have got the point of them all.

Waking to your immediate experience is opening out into space.

The movement of opening naturally touches your heart, evoking some sense of 'Ah!'

Honour 'Ah' – the natural sound that expresses wonder and resolution.

Use questions such as 'what is this?' to help the process of wondering.

Let wondering expose hidden assumptions. As they fall away, notice the sense of 'Ah' as of a penny dropping.

Rest in 'Ah!'—the primordial sound of Reality itself.

Chapter 7: Developing Insight

Examining the Space of Awareness

The Vipashyana aspect of the practice comes in as we begin to wonder what our experience actually is in itself. We do this by wondering what is the mind, what is a thought or a feeling, what is a sensation, what is the space of awareness in which all this happens, who am I, who is it that knows all this, what is knowing and so on.

Wondering here doesn't mean looking for a pat answer or an intellectual theory. It means generating a sense of wonder. When we wonder about something we let it be as it is and appreciate its nature in the immediacy of our experience. We know what we are wondering about directly without words, although words can point to the experience and they often bubble up from it. Sometimes as we wonder we do use a few words, but wondering is not about giving oneself a verbal answer. It is a kind of exploration and process of discovery that happens in our immediate experience, bringing it to life and suffusing it with new significance.

This wondering typically takes the form of deep questioning. For example, you might ask yourself from time to time, what does 'space of awareness' mean? Is space in the mind or is the mind in space?

Insight or understanding begins with a simple sense of movement towards what is fundamentally true. We are drawn towards it by a kind of homing instinct. It is an instinctive or intuitive sense of the rightness, truth and even beauty associated with that. Perhaps the words goodness and well-being come to mind, although sometimes what feels right is sometimes the opposite of what we might normally regard as a good feeling. Maybe aliveness is a good word for what it is we home in on. It is not an opinion about what 'feels right', but a deep sense of having found something of ultimate value, even if only momentarily. As we open our hearts and as we gain a shift in perspective, that homing instinct becomes an understanding that dawns on us. It seeps, sometimes even floods, in and can change our whole perspective.

Insight is associated with a kind of opening movement that we can use to steer ourselves along. It is a natural movement within our awareness. It is like scratching an itch. We home in on it and know it when we hit it, but we have no idea how we do that. As we hit the right spot something happens. The way understanding comes to us is rather like that. We do not manufacture it and we cannot control it. It is just there and we discover it. Vipashyana meditation is both the wondering and questioning, as well as the dawning understanding or realisation.

It is important to deepen and expand your experience and understanding of space and openness in meditation.

(talk to your Mentor and with me from time to time as you work through the course to try to)

The space that is being referred to is nothing other than awareness itself. If it were other than awareness, the question would be how awareness could become aware of it. This takes a great deal of pondering about. If we try to 'see' or sense what awareness itself is, it is elusive for the simple reason that we are our awareness and that everything we experience is in our awareness. To become more aware of awareness means to be aware of the mysterious sense of space in which everything in our experience is happening.

'Let go into space on the out-breath' is a very strange instruction really. It is given to inspire you to explore an aspect of your experience that might have otherwise escaped your notice.

Some people find that the instruction gives them an immediate, intuitive sense of meaning that they want to explore; they find they can easily go along with it. Others find they need more instruction right from the start. It is important to ask any questions that you feel you need to ask at this point, from either your Mentor or teacher.

Everyone needs to come back to the teacher at some point to talk about their practice, but as long as you feel you have plenty to be getting on with, you do not need to ask again until you have given the first instruction a good try. In this way you get a chance to explore your experience before asking any more questions. It is by reporting on what happens when you do this that your Mentor or teacher is able to help you further. When talking to your Mentor or teacher it is important to keep the discussion focused on what you personally find happens in your experience. It is not a matter of trying to make something happen but of becoming clearly aware of what is going on in your experience.

Letting Go and Letting Be

The process of awakening by meditating in this way liberates us and brings out all our wonderful Buddha qualities. This happens by recognizing the true nature of thoughts and of awareness. That is why it so important to appreciate the quality of thought itself, regardless of its content, and let it be.

So, although at first it is a matter of treating all thoughts as equal, almost dismissing them as 'just' thinking, gradually this is replaced by a genuine interest in the nature of thought itself.

When we are lost in thinking, we make all sorts of assumptions about the nature of thoughts. Before we can explore these assumptions we have to learn to acknowledge thoughts as thoughts and let them all go. In other words, we have to give up our attachment to the content of what we are thinking about.

The difficulty in doing this is that habitually we get taken in by our thoughts and become lost in the worlds created by thoughts,

emotions or sensations, rather than appreciating the immediacy and freshness of the ungraspable nature of experience.

At a certain point, the practice becomes more one of letting be than of letting go. It is a matter of letting experience be as it is without complicating it further. This is what happens when you let go of complicating and distracting thoughts. As you let them go you sense a kind of opening movement and that becomes increasingly relaxed and spacious.

This opening happens naturally as you become more familiar with the nature of thoughts. At first they seem to be something quite tangible that get in the way of the meditation. But gradually it starts to dawn that the nature of thoughts is light and spacious. They are not anywhere, they are not anything, they don't stay anywhere and they don't block anything. So what is there to let go of? When you understand this you can just let them be.

Then instead of trying to let thoughts go and then returning to the breath you could notice that nothing ever really moves or goes anywhere. So you really can just let thoughts be. By doing this, one is naturally resting in the spacious immediacy of the present experience whether one returns to the breath or not. There is no need to do anything.

The separate instructions such as 'connect to the heart',' be fully present' or 'opening into space' and so on, are not necessary. All of that naturally happens as we relax. Instead of looking for something to do, such as something to let go of or something graspable that you can come back to, just let be in the natural space of awareness. Awareness is itself naturally spacious. So now all that is required is to wonder at that spacious nature. What is its significance? What is it? Where is it?

What is Vipashyana Meditation Exactly?

You may be thinking that you have no idea what all this space of awareness stuff is about. On the other hand, you might have an intuitive sense of the space of awareness right from the start. Either way, we all need to look again and again at the nature of our experience to realise what it is we are really intuiting and what the significance of that is. Actually the path of Awakening is about recognising the significance of very simple and obvious things. Wondering about what this space of awareness is and what thoughts are and so on is a much more profound way of practising than merely letting go of thinking and coming back to the breath.

To start with, the things that we notice and let go of are distracting thoughts about the past and future, our hopes and fears, ourselves and others and so on. We might be fantasizing, daydreaming, planning, imagining best and worst scenarios, problem-solving, puzzling over strong emotions or strange sensations and so on.

By simply noticing and letting go of the thoughts floating through our mind we can arrive at a state of relative calmness and stability which is called Shamatha. As mentioned in the introduction, although this stability is a welcome relief and can even be blissful, it is not the goal of Buddhist meditation because it does not cut to the root of suffering; the deep misunderstanding of the nature of our being that is at the root of all our problems. We are still trapped and locked into a false view of reality that makes us vulnerable to suffering at every turn. To find the happiness we long for in our heart of hearts we have to go deeper than a temporary state of peace.

This is not to say that Shamata is not useful and important in the development of insight. Indeed, it is the foundation for it. We have to have enough stability to focus on the immediacy of our experience in an insightful way. The insight allows us to spot false views that we take as given, such as our underlying assumptions about the nature of space and time, self and other, our lives and this world. These all form our background worldview and they are how we think the world actually is. As we practise more and more we gradually notice how all we took for granted or as given is just a kind of background thinking. This includes the 'me' that is watching and commenting on all this. It is 'thinking', too.

It is a bit of a shock to realise that so much of what we take to be ourselves, all that stuff that somehow carries the flavour of 'me', is actually thinking. The interesting thing is what happens when you turn towards all that as 'thinking' and open to what lies beyond it. That is a much deeper form of letting go and is Vipashyana, since it involves actual insight.

This process of constantly wondering about our experience, appreciating it, being interested in it, and investigating it, are what allows insight and understanding to emerge. It is strange and could even be scary to find ourselves completely puzzled about things we have always taken for granted, to suddenly realise that we do not understand our own experience. Actually those moments where we realise that we have been wrong in our previous assumptions are moments of clarity; they are nearer to Vipashyana than to confusion.

Vipashyana uncovers the fundamental thinking processes that shape our whole existence. This uncovering is what penetrating insight or understanding is. As we let go more and more, we become aware of ever subtler and more fundamental ways of thinking that lurk in the background of our awareness. The subtler they are, the more fundamental and imprisoning they are. The longer we practise the more aware of these we become and this is how we learn to let them go.

Shamata and Vipashyana Together

The instructions to wake up, connect to our heart, be fully present, and open out into a sense of space lead to both Shamata and Vipashyana. By letting go of distracting thoughts we arrive at calm, and by letting go into the space of awareness, understanding or insight can start to grow. Connecting to the heart brings deep emotional responses, touching on our basic sanity and brings stability as well as understanding, as does being fully present in a relaxed and confident way. Simultaneously, the one simple practice of letting go into space on the out-breath into space uses all the different facets of awareness that are conducive to Awakening.

There are many advantages to this approach. If one does Shamata on its own, trying to stabilise the mind before trying to deepen one's understanding, lots of doubts about the purpose of the practice can undermine one's motivation. If one is wondering about the nature of what one is discovering as one lets go of distractions, this introduces an element of interest and curiosity that has its own energy and motivating power. Each time we get a sense of something genuine and true about the nature of our experience, the more motivated we are to continue to let go of distracting thoughts.

The fundamental instruction to 'let go into the space of awareness' is open-ended. As your understanding deepens, it leads into a meditation that combines both Shamatha and Vipashyana.

The Process of Reflection - What is reflection?

Reflection is an important part of deepening your meditation practice. This can be linked to a teaching you have heard or experience you have noticed that you want to reflect on. What does this mean?

Reflection is different from trying to absorb information or trying to learn something. It is a matter of, for example, reading or listening to a teaching and then thinking about what it means. You have to be attentive and interested, as if listening to something you know is very important, that you know you have to take to heart.

One way of doing this is to do it just after you have been meditating. You ask yourself, 'What does this mean?' It might help to imagine that someone has asked you what it means and so you are trying to tell them. As you do this you may find that you realise you don't understand it at all. Then go back and question whether there is some part you understand, even though you don't understand all of it.

Then relax for a while, allow some space, and then read the piece again. Tell yourself, 'I must think about this some more'. Don't let yourself get angry or despondent, thinking that you are no good because you can't understand or the whole thing is no good because it's all too difficult or unclear. Instead, keep coming back to it and trying to get as clear as you can about the bits you do and don't understand. You might try to work out the reasons for this.

You might find that as you reflect like this, always checking everything with your own personal experience, the amount you understand is increasing by itself. Or you might not. Whichever is happening, you will eventually find you are clearer. You are either clearer because you understand more and it all starts to make sense and seem relevant to your life, or it is clearer because you realise that this is not happening.

You may already be in the habit of reflecting to yourself at odd moments of the day. For example, when you relax into a walk, a cup of tea, or waiting for a train, you might naturally start to reflect. Insights and flashes of understanding can start to pop into your mind at any time, such as in the bath or on the underground. They tend to come unsought, because when you are struggling to find the answer to things you tend to be too strongly focused in the old pattern. It is when you let go of the focus, after having focused strongly on a question that the insight might suddenly pop up from nowhere.

It is important to notice this and realise that it is not coming from a grasping ego-effort. We usually try to grasp at understanding as it comes to us. If we didn't grasp, maybe even more understanding would come to us. That is why the instruction is always to stay open. Even if you do not understand something, you can still stay open and clear about it. By staying open and clear, an appropriate response will pop up. It always does eventually because that is our nature.

Often it is during the meditation session itself that insights and understanding pops up most strongly. We are very attentive and interested in our experience and as we let go of the focus. As the attention drifts, there is a kind of gap or space, and if we don't grasp onto the thoughts that come up, if we let them be without getting involved in their content, suddenly there is a little flash of understanding or a shift in perspective that makes things seem different somehow. Maybe nothing changes particularly, but suddenly what was a problem is no longer a problem, or what seemed opaque now seems clear, or what seemed irrelevant or meaningless suddenly seems significant and means something to you.

This kind of thing is naturally going on all the time, without our having to do anything about it. The path of Awakening is about setting ourselves up in a way that helps this process along.

If this kind of thing happens as you are sitting in formless meditation, there is no need to block it. You can tell for yourself that this is helping to deepen your meditation practice. But then you suddenly notice that you have taken off into speculation or thinking and that it's not at all about your direct experience in meditation any more. As you notice this, come back to the breath. It is important not to confuse meditation with simply sitting there thinking. It is a subtle distinction and you need to make sure you have got the right touch with this.

How to do These Reflections

In all of the reflections in this meditation course, don't let these questions carry you off into intellectual speculation. Use them to home in more directly on your actual experience. You don't need answers in words. You know the experience before you find the words, so savour that experience and wonder at it. Let it communicate its meaning to you in a wordless way.

You can reflect from time to time during the day. You might try sitting with it for a few minutes when you wake, one time during the day, and one time at night before going to sleep.

These reflections are as engaging for a complete beginner as they are for a seasoned practitioner. There is some intuitive sense of meaning in the words themselves and anyone can notice that they correspond to something real in their experience. As time goes on one begins to wonder at the depth of experience revealed by those initial intuitions and to engage in the long process of discovering what, exactly, they are about. It takes a long time to connect to what we are intuiting and even longer to learn to trust that.

If you are completely new to meditation, you might find just the first one or two questions of each exercise quite sufficient to focus on for the whole week. The subsequent questions are meant to help give you a sense of where that first question might lead.

Reflection One: Wake up into your immediate experience

We begin with an intuitive sense that we could be more awake and that this would be good. We can intuit what it means because we never actually lose our connection with the state of awakening. We simply forget it and get pulled away from it through the force of habit. We get lost in thoughts of the past and future. But we don't have to get lost like that. Even without knowing what it exactly means, when we say to ourselves something like, 'wake up to your present experience,' it means something. So the reflection for the first week is to explore what it means to you right now.

This is the beginning of the process of waking up to the wonder of the reality of our experience. By trusting this process of waking up more and more and pursuing it, Openness, Clarity and Sensitivity awaken within us as the Awakened Heart itself.

In order to engage more strongly in this process of waking up, set yourself the task of reflecting on what waking up means and keep repeating the instruction to 'wake up' to yourself all day long and notice what happens. You can do this at odd moments during the day when you remember. You can write little notes for yourself and place them on your desk, on your dash board, in your wallet or wherever to help you remember.

Suggestions to help your reflection

Here are some questions you might like to ponder on as you home in on the experience of waking up. You might find it helps to think of the experience of suddenly being woken up by a loud noise, like a tray of cutlery being dropped right behind you.

- Do you let go of what you were thinking?

- Do find yourself more present? More alive? Expectant?

- What happens in your awareness – does it move around within itself to focus somehow on the here and now? Is that a good feeling?

- Do your sense impressions become more vivid? Do you become more aware of colour, of sound, of smell, of your body? Of the environment? Of what you were doing, feeling, thinking?

- Do you want to be more awake? Does part of you want it and part of you not?

- After you wake up, what happens next? Do you drift off again?

- What is the experience of drifting off and not being awake?

- Is there an experience of being half awake? More awake? Less awake?

- What does 'immediate experience' mean?

- Can one be aware of an actual moment?

- How long is a moment?

- Do sounds and visual images, thoughts and feelings and so on come in single moments or does a single moment contain the whole world in its complexity?

- If you could always be perfectly aware of your immediate experience, would the past and future matter?

- What happens when you ask yourself that?

Reflection Two: Connect to your heart

Remembering this instruction alone would be enough if you could really understand and trust it. It would be resting in the Awakened Heart.

We start with an intuitive sense of meaning of the phrase, 'connect to your heart' and work from there. That intuitive sense might be a kind of blankness, followed by all sorts of objections. That is fine. That is exactly what is meant by connecting to the heart. Whatever happens as you think of the phrase 'connect to your heart' is your starting point for exploring your own experience. Do not linger there too long. Don't let the whole thing get complicated. Just touch the place in you that gives a sense of meaning to that phrase and then wake up.

'Heart' is a subject that opens up more and more as our understanding of the nature of reality deepens. However, even before we begin all that, I suspect that you have some intuitive sense that what you value most lies in the heart. So in this reflection, try to find ways to home in on that experience and notice what happens when you do.

Suggestions to help your reflection

- What happens in your awareness when you say 'connect'?

- What happens when you say 'heart'?

- What happens when you say 'connect to your heart'?

- Is it all the same experience?

- Does it matter which you say first?

- Does it feel good?

- If you think of speaking from your heart, how does it feel?

- When you feel confident and strong, how does your heart feel?

- When you think about what really matters to you – how does your heart feel?

Reflection Three: Be Present

This exercise is about the way you are in yourself and in your relationship to your body and the world. Ultimately it's about living the Awakened Heart, being it in all you are, all you do, and all you say.

We express our presence through our body, actions, movements and speech. We express it in our bearing, our posture and the way we do things. Our presence expresses itself in the way we take our place in the world, the way we take our seat. We are not cowed or defeated; we are not ashamed to exist. We take our place with dignity as human beings and we respect ourselves because we respect all human beings.

Being fully present means to be awake, alert, dignified, confident, relaxed and connected. It means being fully present in our body, being physically present, grounded, centred. It means coming down from the clouds, down from the headiness of too much thinking, being firmly and whole-heartedly present, awake and alive. Only being fully present can we respond appropriately to the situation in the world around us.

Suggestions to help your reflection

- What happens when you tell yourself to be fully present?

- Can you think of anyone whose bearing you would like to emulate?

- How does that feel? What effect does it have on your own bearing?

- What is your bearing like when you feel downcast or defeated?

- What happens when you change your physical bearing or posture? Does it affect your whole experience?

- What is the effect of the instructions for the sitting meditation posture?

- What do you notice about your bearing during the day, working, walking and playing?

Reflection Four: Open Out into a Sense of Space

We begin with an intuitive sense of a possibility of an opening movement. Ultimately this movement into ever-yielding space is realised to be the true nature of our being, ungraspable and mysterious.

To begin with we can notice how any sense of opening up or opening out feels. In order to feel free we need to feel some sense of space. Flying freely through sky carries with it an intuitive sense of joy even if the thought of actually doing that is terrifying.

There is a reason why we appreciate a sense of space and freedom. Our experience is inherently spacious and our suffering comes from trying to hold on to things, close down or secure our ground somehow. The strong urge to build up defences and hide behind them is exactly what causes us to feel imprisoned and restricted in the way we live and act.

So the suggestion to open out and turn towards your experience rather than shrink away, to let go into the spaciousness of your experience, is pointing you in the direction of freedom.

It is also pointing you in the direction of truth.

Suggestions to help your reflection

- What happens when you tell yourself to open or to open out?

- Does it affect your awareness? Your heart? Your bearing?

- Does it feel good?

- Do you feel more relaxed and happy?

- Do you feel a resistance to the opening movement?

- Is it in your body?

- Does your mind go blank?

- Do you let go of thoughts?

- Does a sense of spaciousness open up?

- How big is the space that opens up?

- Do thoughts and sense impressions block the space?

Reflection Five: Let Whatever Arises Go

You wake up, connect to the heart, are fully present and opening out for a moment or so, and then somehow you have moved off that place. Somehow you cannot grasp the moment and make it last. There is a focus and relaxation, and in the moment of relaxation more or less anything could happen. Before you know it you are lost in thinking again. You need to intensify your intention to wake up into your immediate experience and then ride that intention. That intention takes you where you want to go even when you are not particularly thinking about it.

You keep waking up to find you have drifted and have to wake up and return to the chosen focus of your practice. This means letting go of any thoughts and feelings in which you may have been lost.

It could be thoughts of the past, the future, daydreams, planning or trying to solve problems; it could be strong emotions such as anger, jealousy, pride, desire, hatred or just general dullness and sleepiness. Whatever has taken you over, you have to let it go and wake up.

It is one movement. Waking up is letting go, letting go is waking up. If when we wake up a bit, we resist letting go – we don't really wake up. If when we let go we don't really wake up, we don't really let go.

Suggestions to help your reflection

- What does it feel like when you tell yourself to let go of what arises?

- Can you let go without waking up?

- Can you wake up without letting go?

- What stops you letting go?

- What is that experience of not letting go?

- Do you want to let go of whatever arises?

• What happens when you do?

Reflection Six: Let Whatever Happens Be

When you have established a regular practice and can sit quietly and contentedly for the whole meditation session, sensing that the practice is somehow working, that it is somehow going in the right direction, you will have touched into a sense of calm. It is as if the passing thoughts and feelings were the waves of an ocean, and yet they don't really disturb the ocean. The possibility exists for the ocean being at peace within itself. When you start to notice this, you can start to reflect on letting be.

When thoughts are viewed as mere distractions and disturbances that stop us from waking up and being present, we adopt a somewhat negative attitude towards them. Sometimes this is helpful to reinforce our intention to wake up to our immediate experience, but at a certain point we notice that the thoughts are actually our immediate experience. They are not anywhere else.

This means noticing the nature of thoughts. That is to say, what a thought, feeling or sense impression is in itself. This is not at all obvious or easy to experience clearly because of the complicated web of thinking we have woven and trapped ourselves in. Nonetheless, we can, from time to time, notice that we are thinking or that we are lost in a strong feeling of some kind, or seduced by the senses and fixated on something. At that time, instead of simply letting go - which slightly favours the state of being free of thoughts - wake up to the nature of the thought or feeling itself and just let it be. You do not linger. You don't get caught up: which means the letting be is a kind of letting go. But it's not pushing away. It is not treating the thought or feeling as if it shouldn't be there. Instead there is a real interest in what it is in itself regardless of content.

It is almost as if you were welcoming the thought or feeling, savouring it and appreciating its quality before moving on. The problem is keeping awake enough to not get immediately lost. At first when you let be, you find you are quickly lost again. Gradually you find you can let be for longer without getting lost and somehow really appreciate the quality of your experience whether thoughts are present or not.

When you have this kind of stability, you can start to introduce the questions into your meditation practice in a gentle way. It is possible to wonder at your experience, what it is, where it is, when it is, how it is. The questions take you more deeply into the experience rather than into intellectual speculation.

In order to do this, you have to let your experience be. If you let go too strongly then there is a bias towards wanting mental calm and a state free from movement. This is to want to freeze your experience somehow. This is not the path to Awakening.

Suggestions to help your reflection

• What happens when you tell yourself to let be?

• Does it feel good?

- What is the difference between letting a problem go and letting it be?

- Does it seem more subtle to let an experience be than to let it go?

- Is it a matter of the right touch?

- Can you be wholehearted about letting be?

- Remember: not too tight, not too loose.

- Precision and gentleness are the keys to meditation practice. It is necessary to have a certain amount of precision and discipline to allow the meditation to happen and thrive, but gentleness is essential so that meditation doesn't become yet another task we must strive to accomplish.

Heart of Meditation Course

Date Course Started	Date Course Completed

Part 1: The instructions and hints – establishing a practice. This insert is a starting place. You are encouraged to use a journal to reflect in more depth.

Area of Meditation	Notes and Reflections
Essence of Meditation	

Sitting Meditation	
Walking Meditation	

Daily Life Awareness	
Establishing a Daily Practice	

Part 2: Deepening your practice

Area of Meditation	Notes and Reflections
Deepening your Practice	
Developing Insight	

Reflections	What were the most important points you took from this course?
	How has this changed your idea of meditation or your practice?
	Did it add anything to your previous understanding of Dharma or meditation?
	If so, can you be more specific?

Notes:

Notes:

Notes:

Notes:

Notes:

Notes:

Notes:

Notes:

Notes:

Notes:

The cover picture is an abstract from a picture called "A detail of 'Primordial Purity, Golden World' by Contemporary Tibetan Calligraphy Artist Tashi Mannox: (photo by Malcolm Payne of Colourfast Imaging) www.tashimannox.com.

Tashi apprenticed under the direction of a master of Tibetan art, the late Sherab Palden Beru. Part of Tashi's training was in the elaborate art of temple decoration, which is the traditionally hub for the Tibetan arts and its deep symbolism.

Since laying down his monastic robes in 2000, Tashi has built on his disciplined training and arising spiritual awareness, formed through years of practising meditation and Buddhist philosophy - to produce a collection of iconographic masterpieces that reveal powerful, sacred themes through the majestic images of Tibetan Buddhist iconography.

Tashi has known Lama Shenpen since childhood.

Publication date - ©2015

Made in the USA
Columbia, SC
04 November 2017